Patsy Anne Bickerstaff's

Images
at
Christmas

Wider Perspectives Publishing ~ 2020
Richmond ~ Yorktown ~ Norfolk

The writings herein are the creations and property of Patsy Anne Bickerstaff, all rights reserved and author is responsible for them as such. Wider Perspectives Publishing reserves 1st run rights this material in this form, all rights revert to author upon delivery. Do not reproduce without permission except where permitted in reviews or educational purposes. Author may redistribute, whole or in part, at will, for example but not limited to submission to anthologies or contests.

Grateful acknowledgment is given to the following publications, in which these poems previously appeared:

Ariel: Servant to the Rabbi (from Reflection In An Innyard)
The Cloak: Advent, After All This Time, Annunciation, Badge of Honor, Blessing For A Friend, Christmas Blessings, Christmas at Grandma's, Christmas Trees, Christmas Wishes, Discovery, Gift, Holiday Letter, Hosanna, In The Middle, Manger, Pegasus, Santa Photos, The Sleigh Speaks, Wish.
Empty Mirror Press: Inn Woman (from Reflections in an Innyard)
Rockingham Magazine: Holiday Greetings
Showcase: Reflections in an Innyard

Copyright © August 2020, Patsy Bickerstaff, Richmond, Va
Wider Perspectives Publishing, HRACandWPP@outlook.com
ISBN: 978-195277323-5

Contents

Dedication i
Foreword ii

The Tree and the Creche	1
Annunciation	2
Planning the Journey	4
Manger	5
Badge of Honor	6
Night	7
After All This Time	8
Advent	9
Discovery	10
Hosanna	11
Christmas At Grandma's	12
Christmas Mailing (1971)	13
Christmas Bells (2002)	14
Christmas Wishes	16
Christmas Trees	17
Ornaments	18
Gift	19
The Sleigh Speaks	20
Holiday Letter	21
Santa Photos	22
In The Middle	24
Christmas Blessings	25

Wish	26
Blessing For A Friend	27
Holiday Blessings	28
Holiday Greetings	29
Tour Guide: Rhine River Cruise	30
Virginia Christmas	31
Tonight	33
Reflections In An Innyard	
(A Christmas Chancel Drama in Verse)	35
From the Author 48	

Dedication

This book is dedicated to you, the Reader,
To my family and my friendship,
and to everyone who cherishes peace, love, and joy

Patsy Anne Bickerstaff

Foreword
by Ann Falcone Shalaski

Throughout her recent collection, Patsy Anne Bickerstaff's eloquent poems calls us to experience, as she did, joy, faith, and wonderment. She shares a treasure trove of Christmas remembrances. We are treated to flashes of humor, brilliant imagery, and a sense of longing for times, long-ago, when children entertained themselves, and adults lingered over Christmas dinners. Memories so tender, tears swell and we are left breathless.

Page after page touched my heart, such as, *Christmas Trees, Blessings for a Friend,* and *Tour Guide: Rhine River Cruise.* Then there are poems that whisper, allowing the reader to savor those moments of nostalgia. Giving us an opportunity to reflect on the things in life that are worthwhile. We see farther and deeper into the workings of Patsy Anne's, heart.

There are so many reason to own, read, and gift someone with *Images at Christmas.* It is written with precision by an author who demonstrates an uncanny ability to clearly recall years of family gatherings and traditions. The sweet ones, and the gosh-awful ones. But always, a subtle reminder from this author that the spirit of Christmas and "home" is within us.

If a writer could select a perfect time to bring forth an uplifting, restorative body of work, the perfect time is here and now. Readers are eager for a sense of balance in this unpredictable, complex world.

Read and feel transformed, as I have, with beauty, purity, and hopefulness written in the language of love. A gift from the heart and soul of a poet, Patsy Anne Bickerstaff.

Ann Falcone Shalaski
    author of World Made of Glass, Without Pretense, and Just So You Know

The Tree and the Creche

I
wish
for you
Remembrance,
giving, embracing,
wonder and magic, dreams,
laughter, surprises jingling in
silence of snowfall, Faith caroling joy
in starlit dark, kindness hanging in air
like perfume of cinnamon, friendship strong
as pine, twinkling in a thousand places, Love
rich as chocolate, warm as firelight, soft as
kitten-hopes of children.
I wish
for you
Moments
Like sugarplum dancers,
Days like gifts, tied with
shining ribbon,
A lifetime of
Christmas
mornings.
I
wish
for you
peace, good will,
blessings from the
powerful hand of the Infant in a manger.

Images at Christmas

ANNUNCIATION
(after the painting by Luca Giordano, 1632-1705)

I still remember --- startled by the light,
the form that shimmered in my shadowed room,
the roar of words I scarcely understood,
I felt, beneath my feet, the stinging shards
of dreams, of all I'd promised to myself:
a gentle future, with the artisan
to whom I was betrothed; peace, dignity,
a treasure-house of polished furniture;
children in crafted cradles; table spread
with dainties on its perfect surface; toys
sturdy enough for years of robust play;
perhaps a chance to pass a kindness on:
bread for a widow, rest for pilgrims' feet.

How would I manage? I would be alone
to raise a child, in shame I never earned,
discarded by the man who looked on me
so tenderly, but would not comprehend.
How could I tell the world? Or tell my Son
His destiny, teach and protect? My heart
felt frozen. Though I knew I could refuse,
I thought of disobedience, of Eve,
of shattered paradise, and painful earth.
The Presence whispered to me, "Have no fear."
I warmed with courage. Knowing, even then,
that I could not imagine all the grief
in store for me, I answered, "Be it done."

Now, even after all these brutal years,
all sorrow I have dreaded, felt and seen,
as pilgrim, widow, mourner, I can say
without regret, I would accept again,
even the sight of those bewildered eyes
before my husband realized; hiding
that precious Child from savage enemies;

even the strangeness of the things He said;
even the tears I shed beneath that cross,
to hear that angel's word beside His tomb,
to see Him vanquish sin, and conquer death;
to know, as I have known, the love of God;
to love a Son, who loves His Father's world.

Planning the Journey

Her house is here; her table, and the box
for jewels he has promised her "someday;"
the cradle, her beloved family.
Much must be left behind. A donkey's back
can only carry so much weight. Their cloaks,
whatever money they have saved, and this:
the little blanket that her mother wove,
to warm the Child that God will send the world

She fills the pack, makes visits, and accepts
some dates and figs, a little jug of wine
for "just in case." They join the caravan,
start on the road. Her soul rests light
as sunshine, heavy as the universe:
This is the journey that will change the world;
the door to danger, sorrow, pain and joy;
the promise to all generations' hope;

A journey to a stable in the dark,
to songs of angels, and a star's pure light,
to faith and love that live through painful hours
to build a victory for weary souls
brought to the peace and grace of God's own heart;
This is the Christmas journey, always new:
this is the journey to eternity.

Manger

This trough will serve, as it serves ox and sheep.
Rough wood, gray, worn by chins and teeth,
it wobbles, sags a little underneath,
but it can give a Child a place to sleep.

The carpenter can only shake his head;
the cradle, left at home, is finer wood,
smooth, polished, sturdy – why is it not good
enough to be the precious Infant's bed?

Accepting what he cannot understand,
preparing what he finds for nobler use,
he checks for splinters. Where a nail is loose,
he pulls it, lest it scratch the Baby's hand,

and weeps, not knowing why. Yet, from this birth,
this manger will become a holy thing,
become the shining throne of Heaven's King
and feed, not beasts, but hungry souls of Earth.

Badge of Honor

They say, one *other* mother heard her sigh:
so young, so weary, frightened, far from home;
no cradle for her Baby, only hay
that scratched His newborn skin, and made Him cry
and shiver, in the desert's cold night air.
They say that other ears heard his distress:
agile paws whispered on the stable floor,
a striped shadow sprang; two green eyes glowed
above the manger's edge, piercing the night.
The creature picked her way through musty dark
to lie beside the Boy; warm, soft and small.
Her light fur nestling gently on His skin,
she purred the lullabye her kittens loved.
the Infant closed His eyes, and dreamed sweet dreams.
the story goes, His grateful mother reached
to touch the tabby's face, and left a gift –
A grateful mother's blessing, where she touched:
her own initial – blazoned on its brow.
The legend is a pretty myth, and yet
there is no tabby born without that "M".

Night

Dark in the desert, silence breaks only with a jangled bell,
plod of camels' feet thudding on sand,
breath, fogging in nightwind,
Small white gleam guides: star fading into distance.

Dark in the castle, stone, pitch, and black cedar;
dark in a king's cruel soul, smoldering
with vengeance, hatred, anger. Dark eyes squint
to hide the emptiness, the evil inside.

Dark in the mountains, shepherds huddle
between dogs and sheep, clutch the mercy of wool.
a single lamb's cry, like a shard of ice
pierces cold, melts in notes of faint song from blackness..

Dark in the village; travelers cluster, obey
royal edict; fear; instinct to survive;
squirm, shiver on straw, make space.
Tired eyes fall shut.

Dark in the stable, animals, whispers: one woman, one man
The star approaches: blaze of light; Infant's face:
angels and glory; brilliance and music, hope and overwhelming love
From a Kingdom not of this world.

After All This Time

After all these years,
like children, listening
for bells jingling, watching for sooty footfalls
stamping midnight carpets,
we await the miracle
we know to expect.

After all these decades,
like mothers, unfolding crayon artwork,
pressing dandelions in bibles,
we pray thanks for gifts,
prizing most the gift of love,
heartspring of giving.

After all these centuries,
like magi, tracing starcharts,
we remember,
return, wondershocked, to this rough place,
this desert stable,
look on this sleeping Child's face,
baby hands holding our souls.

We stand on tiptoe,
balance on millennia we have climbed,
peer over time's dark lip
into tomorrow's shimmering,
truth gleaming white,
myriad prismed refractions of eternity,
to the same Child's face,
same gift,
same love,
same miracle.

Advent

Oaks' and maples' carnival dresses
curl, brown, tatter at their roots;
bare limbs trace
filigree patterns on pewter clouds.
Laughing stream slows, hushes
to frosty whispers, in and out, between
chill stones, shadows cast by dark pines,
even salamanders on tiptoe.
Murmuration of starlings
writes a secret in disappearing distance.
Winterhawks, like iron statues, gaze hours
for traces of motion.
Muffled crumbs of laughter
fade in silence.
Like notes of harpstrings
vagrant snowflakes flutter and vanish.
Wind holds its breath.
The universe waits for a miracle.

Discovery

Somewhere in the soul
Wonder finds the instant
of life, as when a snowflake,
lace crocheted by the tiniest of angels,
comes to rest; its crystal facets glitter,
perfect star, on night air's
velvet surface,
just as it settles, before it melts
or hides in a crowd
that blends and covers.

The instant is a gift,
flash of hope in wilderness,
glorious in its onlyness, eager
to be part of forever;
to be a lightspark
in an owl's eye, or over a treetop;
icebite on the back of a hand;
a drop of water
on a deer's tongue.

The gift is a Child;
new, perfect, strange,
still familiar, ancient ---
promise and fulfillment;
beginning and completion,
that smiles before keepers
of wisdom, who come with gifts,
seeking him through sandblown days
and shivering nights; who see
His face in the faces
of all children ever born.

Hosanna

In dark,
in silence,
desert village,
a speck in sand;
behind a dim inn,
in animals' stable-cave,
a sound, almost imperceptible
awakens. A single star, moving
across black sky, trails a swath of
sparkling light. Wings flutter, harps,
bells, trumpets, voices, open in a joyful
Alleluia! to unsuspecting earth, Every known
sound becomes a hymn of thanksgiving. Every
color startles, shimmers, refracts, reflects all praise,
all glory, all beauty, all brightness, all infinite love.
The Master of every stone, every light; Lord of all trees,
flowers, waters, wind, every bird, every animal, every soul,
body, mind of every human, Source of all wisdom, goodness,
mercy, laughter, brotherhood, has folded miraculously,
swiftly, silently, unaccountably, into the form of this
gentle infant, magnificent gift, so much more than
the earth could ever deserve or imagine. Let every
sound ring into the universe now and forever; let
every light shine forth celebration, and humble
gratitude, and adoration. Let every bee hum;
every bird carol, every living creature rejoice;
every spirit rise to proclaim the glory of His being.
Let every knee bend at the side of the manger,
all hands clasp in worship, all lips
tell the story forever, the story
of healing in a wounded
world, of hope and
love and new life
beginning in peace,
from silence,
from dark.

Christmas At Grandma's
(*a memory*)

We come from Church to Grandma's house; our ears
still warm from carols, and the words of Luke;
wearing new clothes, and clutching favorites
of new toys Santa left for us at home,
too wonderful to leave alone all day.

Her magic weaves a fragrance in the air
of baking, roasting, lemon, cinnamon;
It blends with cedar- smell – a Christmas tree
alive with colored bubble- candle lights –
and greets the friends and cousins at the door.

At seven, I am old enough to help:
Now, rolling balls of dough in cloverleaves,
and standing on a stool to rinse dark kale
in her white kitchen sink, I know the pride
of nurturing, creating – "woman's work."

The feast will last all afternoon; the guests
will come and go, with gifts and stories, laugh,
remember Christmases from other years,
and faces they will only see again
in Grandma's smile, and soft words to their souls.

The gifts are treasures: boats and bears, a doll,
a locket, and a book –"Little Red Hen;"
a story with a lesson I have learned
already, as I watched my Grandma's hands:
A woman really *can* do anything.

May Christmas bring God's joy in every way,
heal bitterness of winter, hate and fear,
bring memories and hopes and kindest loves,
sunshine and music, laughter and new dreams;
and may there be a Grandma in your heart.

Christmas Mailing
(1971)

The gifts are wrapped and ready, all but these---
These brown ones, most important, must be sealed,
Carried to the parcel post, and mailed.

That's for Kathy; it will cost
To send that heavy book, but how she reads!
I wonder how her mother is; we had such fun
Giggling over childish things,
Sharing high-school heartbreaks.

This is Andy's -- "Fragile, do not scrunch!"
A thousand miles gone,
Andy will laugh at that, even alone.
He won't be home this year;
He has no one at home to see.

One for a brother, and his wife;
He can't leave the base to fly
So far, and back,
But we can love long-distance.
They have each other, mountains, and the snow.

Nothing for Captain Jim, a world away---
Even letters are forbidden, even cards.
Carole can write for us; he has our prayers.
Even imprisoned, he's alive; perhaps next year---

Someone is always away from home; she was.
Tired from the trip, and cold,
She was so young, and probably afraid---
No mother, sister, friend to comfort her,
The beautiful new cradle left behind---
Nobody sent her a gift.
It might have been nice
To have something new for the Baby.
but there was no parcel post
And it was so far from home.

Christmas Bells
(2002, upon Henry Wadsworth Longfellow)

       I heard the bells on Christmas Day
At Ground Zero in New York, in the Potomac
lapping Virginia shores,
         Their old, familiar carols play
To a Guatemalan orphan, a Kosovar widow,
           And wild and sweet
As a prayer for liberty in a Rwandan slave-child's
eyes, or muffled in a burqa,
           The words repeat
Like monks chanting in Taiwan, China, Tibet,
          Of peace on earth
In deserts and rainforests, city streets
and alleys in the projects,
           good will to men
Struggling to know their God, their children,
their brothers, themselves.

        And in despair I bowed my head,
Wept for little girls in Thailand and Ethiopia,
little boys in Pakistan.
        "There is no peace on earth," I said,
Only oppression in Cuba, druglords in Colombia, starvation in
Chechnya,
           For hate is strong,
Greed, addiction and fear still stronger;
the evildoer ridicules God,
          And mocks the song,
Faint, wispy, forlorn,
          Of peace on earth,
Even earth blessed by footsteps
of the Prince of Peace,
           Good will to men
For whom the spirits of Sarah and Hagar grieve.

                    Then pealed the bells more loud and deep
Than a Belfast piper, a Dublin tenor.
                            God is not dead; nor does He sleep,
But smiles from eyes of a Santa,
mourning his sailor son, but bringing joy
to the ill and poor,
                                     The wrong shall fail
At the hands of quilters, making gifts
from memories; of children dropping coins
in red kettles,
                                     The right prevail,
In arms of mothers and foster mothers,
sharing embraces; ordinary men sharing life's blood
                                     With peace on earth,
And in the sky, where old enemies
become new friends, in their man-made stars,
                                     Good will to men
And to women, and children, whose dear faces
shine with the hope and promise and beauty
Of the precious Baby
Whose birth we celebrate.

Christmas Wishes

Christmas
Is bells, carols, colored lights, children, gifts, Santa Claus,
Warmth of humanity that embraces every celebration.
I wish you this.
Christmas
Is silence made sweeter in soft breaking,
Angel's hymns, promise, treasure from God
In a manger remembered forever..
I wish you this.
Christmas
Is a black-green forest, sparkling with ice;
A clearing, snow-blanketed meadow,
One heaven-reaching evergreen, and above it
One clear white star,
A message from my spirit to yours.
The message is this:
You were placed near me
That our lives might touch.
You have comforted me, prayed for me,
Encouraged, taught, and helped me.
You have given me cordiality, kindness,
Knowledge, wisdom, joy.
You have made me laugh, made me think,
Made me brave, made me strong,
Made me something better.
You are what I celebrate in Christmas.
You will always be
Part of who I am.
You are my family,
My friend,
My neighbor.
I will always love you.
God bless you.

Christmas Trees

We measure our lives in Christmas trees;
Sort memories of fir fragrance, pine perfection,
Glitter of aluminum.
We laugh again, at dragging a cedar
In snow and woods,
Plucking a cat from depths of spruce,
Sweeping glass and tinsel
From the one that toppled.
We open boxes, handling angels, gleaming globes,
Mysteries of childhood art,
Santas and strings of beads.
We open hearts, unfold tissue of years
From old affection, friendships, joys,
The true gifts.
We arrange them like toys around the trunk,
A bounty of treasure.
Each tree is every tree,
In its multicolored halo,
Surrounded by love
That lives beyond life,
Knows no time nor distance,
Distills promise from sorrow,
Rainbows from darkness,
Majesty from a Child
Asleep in a stable.

Ornaments

They shimmer, shine, twinkle, glow, sparkle.
They sing, hum, chime, trumpet, jingle.
Scented with evergreen, bayberry, leather, wood, incense,
they taste of cinnamon, peppermint, honey, ginger, cranberry.

Hands, hearts, memories, venture into a box of soft yesterday,
lift out children's gilded giggles, jewel-studded old loves,
friendships still vivid red and green, sisters' and brothers' smiles
that glitter and tinkle, fragrant in shadows.

We untangle a rainbow of lights, snow, angels, Santa, stories, legends,
Sugarplum fairy; the Gospel of Luke
from dim corners, from palaces inside us;
sort, dust, polish, bake, wrap in ribbons, hang on limbs of our lives

all we remember, all we hope. Tonight, beautiful in His eyes,
our spirits become ornaments, glisten, dance in dark desert cold
by a stable in a cave, warmed by a Baby's radiance,
where God so loved the world....

Gift

Here is where
we carry all the beautiful
we can make:
All we can paint, write, sing, play,
can dance, build, carve, say,
adoring, to this place,
dim stable in dark,
to this Light
blooming in our being,
this promise,
This Child.

We receive
More gifts than we can give,
Can imagine, hope, plan, wish:
a snowflake,
hushed forest,
bird's carol,
Love's touch,
Child's face:
This Child.

Here is where
we clasp hands,
know He is,
we are,
Love is
The Gift.

The Sleigh Speaks

All I need do is stand,
however faded, cracked,
loose-bolted, boards worn,
in a meadow; wait in cold, weeds, mud,
for the snow.
To old eyes, weathered wood shimmers
like pewter, rusted runners
catch sunset, gleam red; memories
perch in sagging seats.
Boys strap imagined harnesses
to the dream of a horse,
(for little boys, reindeer.)
Girls drape holly and ribbons
made of words, polish me
with laughter, heap smiles like blankets,
wishes like boxes with bows,
dolls, soft things, warm cakes,
puppies and bicycles, in every space.

I slide on blue-whiteness of a road,
or fly past stars, on a wind
born of Christmas carols
on updrafts of magic,
glide at last to the miracle
beyond weariness, age, rust,
beyond magic, beyond imagining,
beyond gifts, dreams, wishes:
starlit Infant, holding hearts
like treasures, bringing
faith and joy, love
and hope.

Patsy Bickerstaff

Holiday Letter

I wish you...

green and crystal mornings,
artistry of icicles, snowflakes, seedpods,
duckwing flutter, cedar and pine, frost and sparrowsong
sharp, crisp on clean air, sparkling with expectation,
footsteps gentle as prayers...

red and golden memories,
laden trees, peppermint, hearthfire, spice-fragrance,
bells chiming, laughter jingling;
packages shimmering with ribbons; surprise and wonder,
childhood relived, more beautiful, more real than real,
new and young forever, Santa Claus, angels...

blue and silver nights,
glistening cities pointing starward,
whispersnow hushing rush and market rattle
one sacred moment, to hear carol music;
steel and glass glowing, whitelight windows,
peace on earth.

gifts:
sounds, smells, tastes, color, glitter,
joys, stories, friendships, hopes.
I wish you most
a small Boy's gift in a distant barn.
I wish you love.

Santa Photos

They have squirmed in lines
three, four lifetimes long
to perch on the lap
of the same old Saint:
velveteen dresses
with Irish lace collars;
crisp white shirts,
miniature bow ties,
generations of wide eyes
waiting to make
a wish.

Year by year, photographs
collect in albums,
boxes, cards; smile,
almost indistinguishable.
Here, an elf poses,
there, young Mama peers
over a red shoulder at her heart's
treasures, cradled on soft knees,
begging a doll, pony, Red Ryder
Radio Flyer, X-Box, Webkins.

Scattered by years,
miles, life, death,
all the children we have known
or mourned, or cherished,
all the children we have been,
unite by magic of cameras,
by stories passed down centuries;
laugh as one, like music
of bells, carols, glimmer
of stars, toys, lighted trees,

share memories, clasp
invisible hands, and praise, rejoice
to celebrate the birthday
of the Child Who lives forever,
manger-Baby, or Boy who spins
His dreidel, as
He spins the universe.

In the Middle

Right in the middle of shopping and scurrying,
Wrapped in a rattle of scrambling and worrying,
Card-writing, caroling, toy shops and trim-a-tree,
Jingle bells, jangled brains, lives out of symmetry,
Crushed in the rush of frenetic December,
Whispering wings sing, "Remember! Remember!"
Star from the depths of the darkest of blueness
Shines for a Baby, for promise and newness.
Sleeping in silence, the soul will awaken
To peace, love and hope, with its faith yet unshaken;
Rise to rejoice again, musical, lyrical;
This is the magic! Oh, this is the miracle!

Christmas Blessings

The spirit warms its hands
in familiar laughter.
Colored glass yesterdays hang,
like shining fruit, on boughs of memory.
Tomorrows twinkle
in evergreen recesses of hope.
One season, magic
is gifts of snowflake moments: hold a door,
call a friend, smile;
or secret kindness, gingerbread-sweet:
coin in a kettle, doll for a girl
whose toys are twigs and mud.
One night sky hints
a sleigh across the moon,
that star's reflection.
One morning,
feel means believe means know.
We are all children, but this time
wise children, good children
receiving a Child's love, giving back
in an old saint's name,
caroling as wings and bells.

Wish

Once again, in white hush,
In sky-darkness dusted with ten billion stars,
in jangle of bells and clatter of rushing,
windows like beacons, moonsilvered forests,
in sharp green smells, ruby- ribbon tastes,
expectant squirms of searching,
something grows, swells like light,
reaches heavenward like branches,
opens like petals, sings softly,
fills even the emptiest of souls, touches
hand to hand to heart, breathless, waiting
for one moment, one memory
never old, never worn, however many years
it returns, always clean, crisp, true:
a light glancing in old eyes;
laughter caroling in young voices;
feet that will dance, no matter what;
melody leaping on air;
embrace in a doorway, miraculous word;
one star,
one story,
one Child,
one promise,
one
eternal
Love.

Once again, I wish, I pray
all this to your spirit, your life:
all glory, joy,
peace and celebration,
all promise fulfilled,
all memory and anticipation
radiant in your being
for this moment,
this Christmas,
forever.

Blessing For A Friend

Friendship
is that nature of love
that bonds without jealousy
thrives without demanding
cares without possessing.

A friend is a lighted window
where the mind reaches
to know more than itself,
portal where
universe enters, to meld
with the spirit.

Only from love
can the heart learn to love.
only from friends
can souls understand
difference, and that which transcends;
accept their own fragility,
borrowing a cup of wisdom,
lending a carton of strength;

Only from friendship
Can the self know
that Perfect Friend
Who places us each
in other's lives, Who dwells
in every smile, touch, word, kindness;
in song and stillness and laughter.
Comfort for grief, courage in fear.

This holy season, I pray
all blessings, Friend, for you,
and thanks for the privilege
of a life where you have a home.

Holiday Blessings

Magic dances as toys and fairies
in hearth fires, children clustered like holly.
Laughter's hoofprints pack years,
pathlike, through memories that fly,
drift, sparkle in wind.
Rainbows shine from a miracle's heart,
reach from a dusty manger, glisten
on turrets of tomorrows.
Love jingles sungilt bells, sings
carols sweet as cedar, old
as a star that lights a cradle; brings
gifts of morning, soft
as angel down, silver as chimes,
draped with garlands of hellos,
spangled with faces coming home,
voices remembered.
May this be Christmas.
May this be yours.

Patsy Bickerstaff

Holiday Greetings

Be blessed with memories:
Bells, balsam, cinnamon, cedar,
Hearthblaze carols, plush toys, tinsel icicles;
Hold yesterdays in childhood's hand
Like colored glass bubbles.

Be blessed with hope:
Candles in darkness, children's prayers;
Wishes, promises, ribbon-wrapped gifts;
Tomorrow's eyes shining
Like dawn through frost-printed windows.

Be blessed with love:
Mistletoe and kisses, photographs, mailbox messages,
Banquets, brotherhood, wreaths on doors, laughter;
Moments to embrace
And hold a lifetime.

Be blessed with peace:
Snowfall on fragments from crumbled walls of fear,
Dusky pinewood, dove-wing's whisper,
Sleeping Infant in blue-white starlight;
Good will to men.
Be blessed with Christmas.

Tour Guide: Rhine River Cruise

"This was the hill," he said. "The camps were here – and here."
His arm sweeps left to right, eyes follow; he goes on:
"The night of Christmas Eve – they all were hungry, tired,
had marched all day, knew gravely what they had to do.
but it could wait until the sun rose. Bitter cold
numbed fingers, crept in lungs and ached,-- well, maybe just
a little fire – a chance to open mail, to read
the words of love from home, they knew could be their last."

They knew the distant sound they heard; incredulous –
they stopped and listened: "Stille Nacht, Heilige Nacht…"
echoed across the dark, bounced off the ice and frost.
They answered, "all is calm, all is bright…"
Singing with strangers – enemies – impossible –
a concertina, a harmonica, guitar--
the cardboard sign: "NO FIGHT" where did the others find
the paint? White handkerchief, a soccer ball –
kicking, rolling and laughter in the dark and mud;
a feast – Black Forest Cake, biscuits and macarons,
tobacco, coffee-- shared and passed from hand to hand;
Commands ignored; shots fired, but only at the stars--
a memory only few would live to keep.

"The sun," he says, "would bring the battle. Christmas Day
erased the peace and good will. All the boys were men,
killing and being killed, not understanding why."
He hesitates, and gazes at the visitors
Whose grandfathers had told this story years ago:
"Nobody knows the score – who won the soccer game.
But everyone recalls, after a century
the Carol – Schlaf in himmlischer Ruh
Sleep in heavenly peace."

Patsy Bickerstaff

Virginia Christmas

Highland, Allegheny, Shenandoah mountains
ignite with crystal fire
of firstlight, catching frost-prisms
on each needle of each pine.
Prayers of chimneys spiral through blue
haze; every door that opens,
beckons, with perfumed stories of hunter's prize,
garden's treasures, baker's artistry.
Mandolins and dulcimers carol,
accompany laughter of children.

Albemarle, Henrico, Richmond streets
sparkle with bells, candles, glass, tinsel,
sing Tchaikovsky sugarplums, reed-flutes.
Window-candles, running cedar and holly, frame
tableaux of cousins and grandmothers reciting
memories and histories; old priests
in historic sanctuaries, read again
the Gospel of Luke. Under winter sunflare
in clear cold sky, boys
pedal new bicycles.

Surrey, Patrick, Halifax fields
shimmer gold in dawn mist; deer
and cattle, like shadows of old
friends, graze side by side. Filigree
of oaks and maples traces dove-grey air.
Guitars ring through big farmhouses, with notes
like the first Stille Nacht.
Ham, sweet potatoes, peanuts,
biscuits rolled by a child in an apron,
standing on a wooden stool.

Arlington, Fairfax, Loudoun lights
beckon shoppers. Bells chime
beside red kettles, harmony
with chatter of anticipation, click of heels
past endless displays of gifts. Champagne,
shimmering chandeliers. Green wreaths
on crosses remember centuries of heroes,
cling to hope for Peace on Earth.
Little girls in velveteen dresses
Pose for pictures by the tree.

Hampton, Essex, Accomack stars
flicker on trees; in hands of travelers
at Bruton Parish; in dark skies, hurled
from Wallops Island; glow
in moonlight licking waves. Oystermen
breathe satisfying salt wind, smells
of harvest, in stew and stuffing.
Mothers tell stories of angels and shepherds,
Guide small fingers, gilding and silvering
pine cones and sweet-gum seedpods.

In a nation's birthplace, celebrating
that birth not created, every creature:
every eagle, cardinal, opossum,
whitetail, dogwood, magnolia,
pine and live oak, every mountain, wave, cornfield,
every eye, ear, breath, tongue, hand rejoice
in adoration for the miracle
of this moment, this majestic day.

Tonight

is waiting...
like a father, for his child's drowsy eyes to close;
the child, huddled by the tree, over milk and cookies;
a seer, watching a star in distance;
a shepherd, as light unfolds in black sky;
a maiden, shivering in cave-dark
before her Son's birth;
a world, bruised, bewildered, lost
seeking its way through its own shame.

Tonight
is remembering...
like a grandmother, wearing generations
of laughter like pearls on her soul;
a shopkeeper, setting aside
coats for the shelter;
tradition passed like ornaments, old to young;
a prophet reading fulfillment in an infant's face;
a priest, holding in both hands
assurance from a promise aeons old;

Tonight
is loving...
like fingers clasping with decades' familiarity;
telephone ringing, voices sealing endearment;
lullabye over a manger;
heaven spilling messengers, singing;
indelible story living century by century;
prayer, breaking clamor with silence,
brother to brother, dissolving miles, years, difference;
a star, a cross.

Reflections in an Innyard
A one-act play for Christmas

CAST OF CHARACTERS

AL-AKHMAAL, a camel driver

RUTH, the owner of an inn

REBECCA, a seller of donkeys

JUDE, a shepherd

SIMON, a bellmaker

SARAH, servant to the rabbi

JACOB or HANNAH, a dove-breeder

ACOLYTE, minister or choir member, robed

SCENE: An innyard in Bethlehem, some several years after the first Christmas. RUTH, REBECCA, JUDE, SIMON, SARAH, and JACOB or HANNAH are seated in a semicircle, around a small fire, speaking in low tones. AL-AKHMAAL enters and approaches the group.

REFLECTIONS IN AN INNYARD

AL-AKHMAAL: Good morning, Friends! My name is Al-Akhmaal,
    I am a camel-driver from the East,
    And I have been to Bethlehem before,
    some years ago; I drove a caravan
    Of wise men, who were following a star.

RUTH: My name is Ruth, the owner of this inn,
    The widow of Eli Ben-Lemuel,
    And I recall the year of which you speak;
    It was the census-time. I saw the star
    And where it came to rest. I saw the Child.

REBECCA: I am Rebecca, wife of Samuel,
    A donkey-seller, out along the road,
    And I remember, too, the year you mean,
    A certain odd-marked animal I sold,
    The birth of peace that gives my spirit life.

JUDE: My name is Jude, a shepherd from the hills.
    I shall not soon forget the year, the night,
    The angels, shining with the light of God,
    My fear, and how we came down, sheep and all,
    To see the miracle the Lord had sent.

SIMON: And I am Simon, maker of brass bells;
    I can remember waking in the night
    To hear your strange procession in the street,
    To share the miracle of star, and song,
    And God incarnate in a cattle-shed.

Patsy Bickerstaff

SARAH: My name is Sarah, servant to the priest,
And servant to the priest who came before.
I, too, remember looking at the star.
It was while my first master was alive,
The precious gift we had been waiting for.

DOVE-BREEDER: (Hannah)(Jacob), seller of sacrificial doves;
I know the year, and have reflected much
Upon the time. I also saw the Child,
And sing the praise of God, that I have seen
the revelation of His love for men.

REBECCA: My husband taught me skills of buying beasts:
(stands)   Straight back, tough legs, alert, well-winded, strong,
              Not over-stubborn, neither young nor old.
              We sell our donkeys on the desert road
              And travelers pay much for such fine stock.
              I bargain well as any man, and yet
              He called me fool when I brought that one home.
              Bad luck, he told me. It would never sell.
              He showed me, on its back, the evil sign,
              The stark black cross, etched in its rugged coat.
              I ridiculed the superstitious tales;
              "The God of Jacob, Isaac, Abraham,
              Creates no evil animals," I said.
              "Leave talk of curses for the ignorant
              And if these tourists are afraid of it,
              A healthy ass will be of use to us."
              Brave indignation! Nonetheless, I found,
              Although the gentle creature served me long
              And loyally, the shadow which it bore
              Would haunt me with a nameless, chilling fright.
              The day the strangers came, I sat alone
              Staring across the desert, absent-eyed
              In midday glare, and stroked the donkey's face.
              The quiet man and woman startled me;
              I stood, apologized, brushed off the dust
              and brought the livestock out, for them to buy.
              Speaking in soft accents, among the herd,
              They made their choice. My face went pale with fear
              The woman was to be a mother soon!
              "No! Take another one!" I cried to them,
              "What if this sign of death should curse your Child!"
              Her eyes looked sad one moment, then grew warm
              "The God of Jacob, Isaac, Abraham,
              Creates no evil animals," she said,
              "This little creature cannot curse the Child.
              Instead, perhaps, the Child will bless the beast;
              His birth may make the cross a sign of life."

Patsy Bickerstaff

They bought the donkey then, and went their way.
I watched them disappear, through rippling heat,
And somehow understood. The words were true.
     (Return to place)

SIMON: Some say there is more noble work with brass
(stands) Than making humble bells. I might have been
A craftsman in the palace of a king,
An artisan of temple ornaments
That show my skill, and tell the world my name.
But bells enchanted me for many years;
They fascinated me with form and tone,
Like metal birds that celebrated art
With melody and glitter when they moved.
The songs that bells play are the songs of life,
Strong sounds of working men and animals,
Sweet harmonies of field and marketplace.
Bells chant the coming of the caravan,
Of merchants, with their gems and colored rugs,
Their silks and magic spices, figs on strings.
Bells call the shepherds to their grazing sheep
And ring among the hills when sunset falls.
They jingle joyous laughter for a feast
Like sounds of stars, on dainty dancers' feet.
I never blushed to dedicate to God
The duties of a fashioner of bells,
The worthy task my hands have found to do.
It was the voice of bells that I heard first,
That sacred night when the Messiah came;
The tinkling bells of sheep that filled the street
As shepherds made their way to find the Child;
And in the stable's hush, the only sounds
Were tunkling from an ox that shook its head,
And jangling of some camels' harnesses,
As if the God of Israel ordained
Bell-music to be holiest of all,
As if wherever men proclaim God's love,

      Rejoicing in His gifts to humankind,
      Their song of joy should be the sound of bells.
            (Return to place)

RUTH: A widow in my youth, left with the inn
(stands) And little else, I had no other choice
     But run the place myself. I learned the chores:
     Build fires, fetch water, sweep, stretch lentil soup.
     I shout at those who hesitate to pay
     And threaten those who act disorderly
     With my imaginary husband's wrath,
     Pretending him alive, for safety's sake.
     The work has made me hard, and even crude
     But then, I was no empress from the start.
     Whatever good the census did the king,
     It filled my inn. The room for guests sleeps ten
     But I took twenty. A prolific lot,
     This tribe of David; loud, unruly, coarse.
     I had to turn away the other two;
     What could I do, with people such as those?
     The man had calloused hands, from honest work,
     The girl, her baby due, was gracious, soft,
     The kind of woman I once wished to be.
     I shook my head and closed the door, then turned
     To call them back. I sent them to the barn.
     Was it the star, or song, that woke the town?
     I still recall a midnight turned bright blue,
     Voices that sang, "Glory to God!" and "Peace!"
     The swaddled Infant, sleeping on the hay,
     The soul-warmth, telling me that even I,
     A mule-mouthed harridan, with wrinkled face,
     A heavy chin, thick skin and dusty feet,
     Am not a stranger in the sight of God.
     He knows what He created me to be,
     What sorrows made these lines between my eyes,
     What tears I swallowed, making my throat rasp
     Like ravens gossiping in olive-leaves.
     He feels my burden, understands my pain

And loves me, even in my homeliness.
He finds it beautiful, to hear me sing
With angel choirs, "Glory to God!" and "Peace!"
                          (Return to place)

JUDE: Huddled in night, rough woolen robes pulled close,
(stands)   Low voices cursed cold, darkness, stabbing wind.
Half-sleeping among stupid, wanton sheep,
We thought the light and music were a dream,
A mindfright, born of skimpy meals, rude beds.
It took a moment to believe the sight,
And superstitious fear conceived the doubt
That God would thus invite the ignorant.
I told the others I would mind the herd
While they went to the shining people's child.
But they would have none of it. "Come along!"
And so I went. We led the bleating beasts
Down rockslide path through rabble-ridden streets,
That reeked with noise and smells of travelers.
A strange parade of visionary men,
We wound between the drunken, mocking mobs
Till, in the alley way behind an inn,
We found the cave. A weary-looking man,
His pale young wife and Baby were inside.
We have reflected, over passing years,
It was not what we saw, but what we felt
That gave us wisdom, writing on our souls.
We have reflected, too, on kings who came,
Whose lives were spent in search of what we found,
Their conscientious studies leading them
At last, to where obedience brought us,
To kneel before the cradle of a Boy.
They came with gold; we brought no gifts, and yet
The gift that we received was nothing less
Than theirs; that night remains with us,
And sometimes in the hush of mountain dark,
There is a certain echo in the wind,
A melody we almost think we hear,

And someone's lips will move to form the words,
"Glory to God on high, and peace to men."
(Return to place)

SARAH: For years, I quietly performed my tasks,
(stands) Almost unnoticed in the Levite's house.
I was the only servant; it was hard,
But there was not enough to pay a man
And hands work willingly for one so kind.
At evening, when my brooms were put to rest,
I sat beside his door, to hear him pray.
With sunset through the windows, glowing pink,
And fragrance from the gently burning lamp
I listened to the music of his chant,
To beauty of the ancient sacred words,
And wished this God would hear a woman's prayers.
By day he read the scripture, and I watched
How year by year, his head was drooping low,
His finger traced the words he strained to see.
The day I saw his tears, I shared his grief
And bit my fist to keep from crying out.
How cruel of his God to take away
The holy joy that dear old man had found!
My rage and desperation tore my soul;
The only way to help him was a sin!
Three days I worked in silence, and at last
With timid tones that he could scarcely hear,
I whispered, "Master, let me be your eyes."
I knew it shocked him, but in time he laughed.
He taught me how to read, but made a rule:
I must not read the scrolls, except for him;
Thus, it would be no woman's act, but his,
A rabbi borrowing a woman's sight.
His life went dark; we kept the secret safe,
But failed in hiding from my hungry heart
The majesty that echoed in the words,
The precious promises my eyes had learned.
One twilight, I had led him from his prayers;
The heat of desert day had turned to cold.

I closed the shutters, one by one, until
I reached a little window, facing east.
O Miracle! Made breathless by the sight
I stood immobile, silent for a while,
Then shouted like a girl: "Rabbi! A star!"
His keen ears heard the singing first. He smiled,
Then, with a whispered voice, he joined the song:

"Glory to God," he sang, "and Peace on Earth!"

The recollections sparkle in my mind
Like jewels: how I led him to the place,
His old face wet with tears of happiness,
The holy Child, the privilege we felt,
The memories he cherished all his life.
It may be wrong to let a servant read,
To let a woman see the word of God;
So says the law. But if the Lord, Who knows
All things, has blessed us with such great reward,
Then sharing vision cannot be a crime.
              (Return to place)

AL-AKHMAAL: The trip was long; I was one of the few
(stands)   Willing to come with these astrologers,
           To unknown destinations, with no chart,
           To join a journey led by hope and light.
           Some drivers called the plan a crazy scheme
           But my imagination caught a spark:
           With skin burned tough from sun and desert wind,
           With throat grown dusty from the taste of sand,
           With years of learning all the routes and roads,
           With scores of miles behind me, I was lost.
           I never had direction in the past;
           My weary life had gone so many ways;
           So many goals unmet, dreams unfulfilled.
           Nothing was left to follow but a star.
           There was a spirit in this caravan
           Unlike the others I had always seen.
           It seemed the magic of the old men's dreams

Had filled the heart of everyone who came.
We traveled eagerly; we sang with joy
to rhythms of the camels' plodding feet
And jangling bells. We never cared how long
The ride would be, or where the search would end.
Faith gave us strength. We knew the star would lead,
And so it did, past villages and towns,
Past cities, camps and kingdoms. Weeks, then years.
"A king, and greater than a king," the magi said,
Would greet us when the journey was complete.
There was some talk of riches, grand estates
And royal favors; no one of us knew
How little those would matter, in the end,
How great a privilege would be bestowed.
Each time we reached a castle, rumors hummed:
Was this the place the new King would be born?
Horizons rose and fell; the star moved on
And so did we. At last, in Bethlehem
We found the place; no palace, but a stall,
A stable in a cave. Could we be wrong?
I trembled with uncertainty. The star
Had stopped above this roof. There was a Child,
But where was all the pomp, the majesty?
This manger was no cradle for a King!
Had Heaven played a trick on these old men?
Had I made one more aimless search, and lost?
It could have been an ordinary scene,
Except that it was not. Almost in tears
I looked, and with one glance, my heart knew peace.
Oh, happy eyes, to see the face of God!
Oh, happiest of hearts, to feel His love!
                              (Return to place)

DOVE- BREEDER: (stands)	I am a breeder of the temple doves, Sky-farmer, and a harvester of prayers, An instrument, held in the hand of God, His partner in creation, fashioning With finest seeds and grain, with patient care,

These birds, almost too beautiful for earth.
In gilded mornings, watching day arrive,
I listen to their murmur in my lofts,
A muted song, like messages from God
As when the prophet, coming from the storm,
Found hope in white wings beating on blue sky.
Outside the synagogue, I bring my birds
To sell the faithful, for a sacrifice,
To ask a blessing on a newborn child,
Or offer thanks for fortune, health or love.
The fondest wishes, and the dearest joys,
Beyond expression of the spoken word,
Are carried by these snow-white offerings.
There was a day once, by the temple-gate,
A woman, with the gentleness of doves,
An Infant with the beauty of the dawn.
I spoke of birds, how a dove-keeper's life
Is not without its melancholy times;
One spends so many hours, so much concern
To bring these creatures, pure and beautiful,
Perfect and innocent, as sacrifice
To meet the needs of ordinary men;
Yet there is comfort in the holiness
Of honor, to be giving back to God
His loveliest creation. Then she smiled
And nodded. "Not unlike a mother's work."
Astonished by the simple words, I looked
Into the sleeping Infant's face, and saw
A shining vision of eternal love,
Incomprehensible and infinite.
There were not doves enough to give Him thanks
For what this Child would mean. O souls of men,
Rejoice before the Lord, Who gives us life!
Give praise to God, Who visits and redeems!
                    (Return to place)

(Enter ACOLYTE or other robed figure, carrying a candle. Lights the candle from the innyard fire, and faces the audience or congregation.)

ACOLYTE: "Let there be light." With that first breath of time,
            The Great Imagination willed a dream
            And made it real, and saw that it was good.
            The universe was filled with suns and worlds,
            With moons' and comets' blazing wonderdance,
            Spinning, burnbursting, bright with heaven-fire.
            Then, in the glory of the day He made,
            The joy of God exploded into life,
            With forests, blossom, fruit; clear crystal wings;
            With glimmer-scales, and opal eyes, and best,
            The creatures in His image, given souls
            And dreams, and will, and love; children of dawn.
            So, even in our disobedience,
            In wander-years, the morning was not lost.
            Through centuries of sin, a searing shrub,
            A rainbow's prismed brilliance, lamps unquenched,
            The miracle of light led men to God,
            Told us that He had not forgotten us,
            Had loved us too much to withdraw His eye.
            It was not strange that one majestic star
            Should shine the way across an aching earth,
            Through skies like caverns, over moonpearled sand
            To fade before the Fire of Bethlehem.
            It was by His command, in gray stone hills
            That shepherds' messengers came shimmering
            In mists of iridescent melody;
            That by their nature, men should understand
            And follow, unafraid, through foreign plains
            And villages, to kneel before His Son.
            So we could not forget, in all this time,
            A hundred generations afterward;
            We see Him, and remember, in the flames
            Of candlegleam, and hearthfire; in the glow
            From multicolored windows of His house
            On midnight snowfalls; twinkling trees

And wreaths, star-sparks, and open doors, recall
Desert campfires, torches in catacombs
Where we have shared, and kept alive, the word,
The gospel of the Gift. And even now,
We pass, to children first, this history,
The small refracted stories of our faith
Flaring to one, igniting, with these scraps
Of memory, new wisdom in young hearts,
A message radiant with the love of God
Who, having blessed us into being, once,
Came back to us in dark and wilderness,
To bring us home, to spirit-warmth and life.
So, in the hearts and hearths and minds of men,
Let there be peace, and praise; let there be light.
(Exit, in procession, followed by all other characters.)

From the Author

Whatever time of whatever year you read this book, I wish you a Merry Christmas! These poems have been written over the years, against the background of a changing world, about a season which signifies hope, joy, love and peace, all of which I wish for you, whether you are a believer or an observer of the Christmas tradition.

Let me introduce myself: I am a mother and grandmother, with B.A. and J.D. degrees from the University of Richmond, Virginia. I have studied poetry writing at the University of Virginia, the University of Richmond, Virginia Commonwealth University, and the Bread Loaf Writers' Conference at Middlebury College, Vermont. I have taught poetry writing classes at the University of Richmond's Osher Institute of Lifetime Learning, and at the Peter Paul Development Center, Richmond, VA. I have presented readings and discussions at libraries, churches and schools, and chaired writers' groups. My work has appeared in about 200 periodicals, reviews and journals, in print and online, and has won numerous awards, including the Robert Penn Warren Poetry Prize. I was a three-time finalist for Poet Laureate of Virginia.

A lifetime member of the Poetry Society of Virginia and the Virginia Writers' Club, I served in executive positions in both organizations, including four terms as president of the Poetry Society of Virginia, and one term as president of the Virginia Writers' Club, which awarded me a Lifetime Achievement Award. I have visited England, Tuscany, France, Ireland, Greece, Mexico, Canada, the Netherlands and Germany.

Images of Christmas is my fourth book, my third poetry book, after *City Rain* (Librado Press, 1989) *Chained to a Post* (self-published) and *Mrs. Noah's Journal* (San Francisco Bay Press, 2007) After years of receiving letters of good news, tucked into greeting cards by friends, and appreciating the personal touch, learning about their adventures and milestones, I began responding with a poem enclosed in my cards. This became an annual tradition.

Now, at the suggestions of some friends, I am combining the Christmas-card poems into a book. This little collection includes all the Christmas-card poems I could find, and further includes my Christmas chancel drama, *Reflections in an Innyard*. This one-act play was originally written at the request of a minister's wife, when the children at their church became unwilling to participate in a Christmas pageant, and an adult presentation was being sought. It later received an award from the Shenandoah Valley Writers' Guild, was published in their anthology, *Showcase*, and has been performed at numerous churches, including Old St. John's Church in Richmond, VA.

May these poems provide enjoyable reading, fond memories, understanding and joy in the beautiful story of the Nativity and the incomparable spirit of family, friendship and celebration of this very special and most meaningful season.

Patsy Anne Bickerstaff

www.ingramcontent.com/pod-product-compliance
Lightning Source LLC
Chambersburg PA
CBHW031217090426
42736CB00009B/946